WHAT CAN I DO?

inspiring activities
for creative kids

mary richards

agnes & aubrey

Contents

INTRODUCTION

What will you do today?

Look no further than this book! You'll find plenty of activities to choose from. Take a moment to look though, and decide where you'd like to begin. You can start with the very first activity, 'Create a World', or turn to a random page – like 'Draw a Narwhal' or 'Make a Time Capsule' – and just dive in! There's no special order, and no rules either.

How to get started!

Once you've settled on a page, you'll find it divided into different sections: 'You'll Need', 'Getting Started', and 'Hints and Tips', which will help you make the most out of your chosen project. Some of the activities will work better with a friend (or two, or three), and others you can complete entirely on your own.

A world of wonder

As you read the book, you'll also discover some facts about the activities you've selected. In the 'Did You Know' boxes (on the right-hand pages), you'll notice that many of the games, tasks, and activities have been enjoyed by children across the world for hundreds (and in some cases thousands) of years.

Most of the activities can be done indoors, but there are ideas for outdoor fun too. All you'll need to get started is a pencil and paper – and a lot of imagination.

Have fun!

CREATE A WORLD

You'll need

Pencil & paper

Imagination

Let's invent a new land, and design a set of characters to live in it. You can use the world you've invented as the setting for a story.

GETTING STARTED

Write down your **first ideas**! You can begin by asking yourself these questions:

- **Where** is your world? Is it on this planet or in a fantastical location? What animals or plants are found there?
- **Who** lives in your world? It needs some **characters**! You could draw their faces or describe what they are like.
- Try **drawing a map**. You can invent names for great cities, magical mountains, or rushing rivers.

HINTS AND TIPS

The world could be based on **something familiar** (like your home or school), but you could add a **strange or unusual** element. OR you could create an **entirely new world**, that doesn't look like anything you know! You don't have to finish your world in one go. Keep your notes and drawings in a folder, and add a little more to your world each time.

Incredible adventures might take place in your world!

You could include magical castles, beaches, or lakes.

DID YOU KNOW?

The **Bronte sisters** (Charlotte, Emily, and Anne), who lived in England in the 19th century, wrote many novels including *Jane Eyre* (Charlotte) and *Wuthering Heights* (Emily). Growing up in Yorkshire, with their brother Branwell, they invented worlds called Glass Town, Angria, and Gondal. As well as writing stories and poems about the lands they'd created, they sketched maps and drew pictures of characters that lived there.

PLAY CONSEQUENCES

You'll need

Four pieces
of paper

Pens or pencils

Some friends –
three is best

In this drawing game of randomness and chance, you can create fantastic and wonderful characters.

GETTING STARTED

With the paper in **portrait** format, fold in half, and then in half again. You're going to fill these parts of the paper with your character's **head**, **body**, **legs**, **and feet**.

- Take it in turns to draw one part, then fold the paper over. After you've done this, pass the paper to your friend. Carry on drawing and swapping until you've filled in all the sections of the paper.
- Unfold, and reveal your crazy creations!

HINTS AND TIPS

Leave the bottom of the neck, waist, and legs visible after you've folded the paper. Your friend will know where to connect the part they're working on!

Be detailed! Include hair, eyebrows, a beard, or jewelry.

Your character might like some accessories! They could be holding a fish or riding a skateboard.

You don't have to stick to drawing one head, or two arms. A creature could have two heads, three eyes, and six arms!

DID YOU KNOW?

A group of artists known as the **Surrealists** played this game in their studios and homes in Paris in the 1920s and 30s. They also **wrote stories** as a group, using the same method – taking it in turns to add new words to the text. The Surrealists believed in the power of the imagination, and loved creating art and stories without planning them in advance. They were also inspired by their **dreams**!

INVENT A DANCE

You'll need

Comfy clothes

Space to move

Some music

It's time to make up a dance! Sometimes dancers follow particular patterns or steps. At other times, they move freely, using their imagination.

GETTING STARTED

- First, **warm up** and **stretch out**. Jump up and down a few times. Circle your arms, then point your fingers and toes.
- Find a **piece of music** to dance to. You could play it out loud, or imagine it in your head. Clap your hands in time to the beat so you can work out the rhythm and speed of your dance.
- Decide whether you will dance **standing in one spot** or **moving around** the whole room.

HINTS AND TIPS

Take it **step by step**! Think of all the moves you'd like to make. Practise them one at a time, and then put them all together. You could dance on your own or with a friend.

To inspire your dance you could think of nature - the wind blowing in the trees, or the sea lapping to the shore. Include simple movements like walking, skipping, or rolling in your dance.

You could pretend you're a robot or a puppet on a string and try making quick, jerky actions.

It's fun to combine flowing, graceful movements with still, balancing poses.

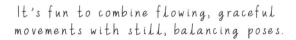

DID YOU KNOW?

Dancing is very old! In the caves of India, **ancient paintings** that are thousands of years old appear to show groups of dancers moving together.

create a boardgame

You'll need

Paper, card & scissors

Dice

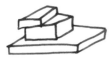

Some board games to look through – if you have them

Board games made with squares, counters, and dice are simple to make - and fun to play, too!

GETTING STARTED

This game is based on **Snakes and Ladders**, which has been played for thousands of years. Players roll **dice** to move their counters across the board – but face many different obstacles along the way!

First, make the **board** and a **counter** for each player. Number your squares from 1 to 36 (add more squares or more counters for a longer game). Draw on **snakes**, **ladders**, and **challenge squares** to make the journey to the end of the board more exciting! Write the challenges (like 'say the alphabet backwards') on a set of cards.

HINTS AND TIPS

You could create more games based on ones you already enjoy. For a simple **memory game**, draw ten (or more) pairs of picture cards. Shuffle the cards and lay them face down on a table. People take turns to turn over **two cards at a time**, keeping the cards if they discover a pair. The trick is to remember where the pairs are hiding!

For this game, roll DICE and move COUNTERS around a board. The WINNER is the person who gets to the end first!

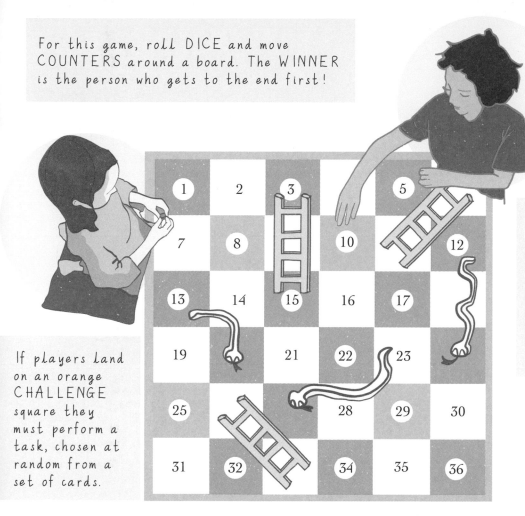

If a player lands on a LADDER they move up the board. Landing on the head of a SNAKE pulls them back down again!

If players land on an orange CHALLENGE square they must perform a task, chosen at random from a set of cards.

DID YOU KNOW?

The Royal Game of Ur is the **oldest board game** in the world. It was played 4,600 years ago in ancient Mesopotamia. Players took it in turns to race counters from one side of the board to the other.

READ A MIND

Pencil & paper

A friend who
wants their
mind read

How well do you know your friends? It's time to find o
You can also impress them with a mind-reading trick!

GETTING STARTED

Think of some **questions** to see how well you and
your friends know each other. Here are some
examples – but you could think of others too.
- What's your **favorite film**?
- What's your **favorite color**?
- Name a **place** you'd like to travel to.
- What **job** would you most like to do?
- What's your **favorite animal** for a pet?
- Name the **food** you love most of all.

HINTS AND TIPS

Write your questions on two pieces of paper. Ask your friend to write **their answers** on
one piece, while you write **what you think they'll say** on the other. Compare notes!
– Next, for a trick that's almost guaranteed to show off your **mind-reading skills**, follow
the questions opposite.

Ask your friend this series of questions.

1   Think of a number between 1 and 10. Don't tell me what it is.
Now, multiply it by 9.

2   Add the digits together. (For instance, if your answer is 45, add together 4 + 5).

3   Subtract 5 from your number. Convert the number you now have to a letter. A=1, B=2, C=3, D=4, E=5, F=6 (and so on).

4   Think of a COUNTRY that begins with that letter.

5   Take the second letter of the country you've chosen. Think of an ANIMAL beginning with that letter.

6   What COLOR is that animal?

The answer you have written down will almost certainly be: A GRAY ELEPHANT FROM DENMARK.

DID YOU KNOW?

Denmark is one of only **five countries** beginning with the letter D, and it's the one that most people will think of when answering this quiz. If they do happen to pick another (or they confuse their numbers), your trick won't work!

write a letter

You'll need

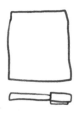

Pen & paper

Envelope

A stamp

Why not write a letter to someone special? It could be a friend you see every day, or someone who lives far away. It's so exciting to receive a letter!

GETTING STARTED

If you know their **address**, you can get writing! You'll want to tell them all your **news**, and ask them a few **questions** too. Why not let them know:
- **What you've done** at school or at home.
- All about any **places you've visited**.
- What are your **hobbies** at the moment?

You could also ask them to share their news with you!

HINTS AND TIPS

Why not include a **drawing** of yourself – or a picture of the two of you together! If you don't have an envelope, you can make one, following this **guide**.

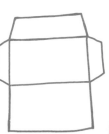

It's fun to draw on the envelope too.

You'll need to attach a stamp and find a place to post your letter! What does your post box look like?

DID YOU KNOW?

The world's **first postage stamp**, which was launched in the United Kingdom in 1840, was known as the 'Penny Black'. It marked the first time that postage was paid by the sender of the letter, rather than the receiver. The stamp cost a penny and contained a portrait of Queen Victoria.

make a shadow puppet

Card & pencils
to stick it to

Scisssors &
tape or glue

A light source
that can be
directed –
like a torch

Create dramatic scenes by making shapes with your hands or cutting out puppet characters.

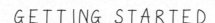

GETTING STARTED

A shadow is made when an object **blocks the path of a ray of light**. Its shape is magnified on the wall.

- Make the room as dark as you can, except for **one light**, or a torch, which you should point at a wall.
- With your hands between the light beam and the wall, try out **different shapes**.

HINTS AND TIPS

You could create more puppets by **cutting out characters** and sticking them to **pencils**.

Some impressive shapes to make with your hands are animal characters: a crocodile, a dog, and a bird. Can you invent any others?

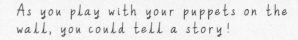

As you play with your puppets on the wall, you could tell a story!

DID YOU KNOW?

In Indonesia puppet shows have been put on for thousands of years. Shadow puppetry is known as **wayang**, which means 'shadow' or 'imagination'. Wayang shows tell stories of myths and legends and are usually accompanied by music of the **gamelan** – an orchestra made up of metal gongs and drums. Performances begin in the dark at midnight and last until the sun rises at dawn the next morning. Puppets are crafted from leather and attached to rods that are operated by puppeteers hiding behind the scenes.

MAKE A DEN

You'll need

Chairs or tables

Blankets, sheets or cushions

A torch

It's fun to create a cozy space in which to read, write, draw – or just relax doing nothing.

GETTING STARTED

Decide **where** you'll make your den. You'll want to choose somewhere **comfortable** and **out of the way**!

- A table or two chairs will make a good **frame**. Drape sheets or blankets to make the **walls**, leaving an opening for a **door**.
- Before you add the finishing touches, make sure you like the **shape** of the den. Check you can fit inside!

HINTS AND TIPS

- Use **pegs** or **heavy books** to keep everything in place.
- A large **cardboard box** could form part of your den.
- You could take a **torch** inside – so you can read or draw when it gets dark.

You could make a sign to invite people in - or keep them out!

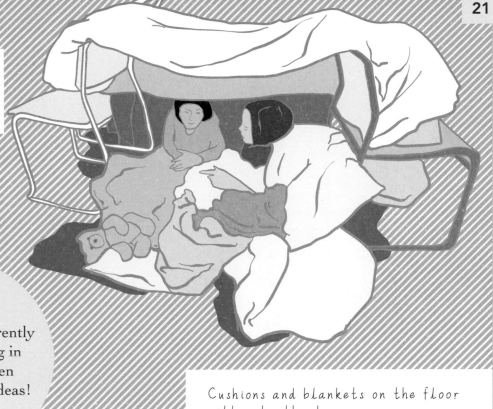

Do you think differently in your den? Sitting in different spaces often brings about new ideas!

Cushions and blankets on the floor will make the den cozy.

DID YOU KNOW?

Wild animals build dens to survive. They use them to store food, raise their young, and shelter from hot or cold weather. **Polar bears** make theirs by tunneling under the ice, where they stay throughout the harsh winter. **Fennec foxes** also tunnel underground. Their desert dens can be up to 70 feet long, and 8 feet deep – this keeps them out of the daytime heat. They use their huge ears to listen to faraway sounds.

create a collage

You'll need

Colored paper

Magazines or photos that are OK to cut up

Scissors & glue

Get out your scissors! A collage is an artwork made from shapes you've cut or pictures you've collected.

GETTING STARTED

Gather old **magazines**, **newspapers**, or **photos** that are not too precious. Cut out any pictures that you like the look of. Once you have at least 20 images to play with, pick your favorites to arrange in a collage. You could combine everything in a realistic way or create something unusual.

HINTS AND TIPS

Organise your images in **categories** – people, animals, birds, objects, backgrounds, and so on. You could **store them** in a box or a folder. When you come to make a new collage, you'll know exactly where to look to find what you need.

Mix different colors and shapes. You can glue them on to a sheet of paper.

Create something extraordinary by combining different photographs. You could put an elephant in a snowy forest with a beach umbrella!

Give your work a title! Cut out letters from magazines and stick them together.

You could make a group of pictures that work as a series. For example - there could be an elephant in all of them!

DID YOU KNOW?

In the last years of his life, the French artist **Henri Matisse** (1869–1954) made many collages or 'cut-outs' from shapes he'd cut from sheets of brightly painted paper. He called this 'drawing with scissors'. With the help of his assistants, Matisse pinned his paper shapes up on the wall to try out different combinations.

INVENT A MENU

You'll need

Pencil & paper

Some food –
for inspiration!

It's time to dream up your fantasy menu.
You don't actually have to make any food
– just let your imagination run wild!

GETTING STARTED

- Is your meal for a **special occasion**?
- Are you planning your menu to be eaten **at home** or in a **restaurant**?
- How many **courses** will you put in your menu?
- **Who** will eat your meal?

HINTS AND TIPS

Draw out your menu on a sheet of paper. You could give your restaurant a **name** and draw its **logo**. Would your restaurant be near your home or somewhere far away? It could be on the moon!

RESTAURANT NAME HERE
LOGO

-MENU-

Starters
You'll want to include a mix of small dishes
to get your guests' taste-buds working!

Main Courses
These larger dishes are the main attraction!
Describe them in an appealing way.

Desserts
Imagine a selection of sweeter treats to enjoy
after the main meal.

Drinks
You could mix juices and slices of fruit to
produce mouth-watering combinations.

Your menu might
be strange -
mixing baked
beans with mint,
custard, and
cheese.

You could give your dishes exciting names, like
Apple Fantastic or A Ceremony of Crumble. They
might one day become famous - like the Hot Dog,
the Caesar Salad or the California Roll.

DID YOU KNOW?

In 1575 a great feast was held in honour of **Queen Elizabeth I of England** at the grand
Kenilworth Castle. Guests dined on 300 dishes including sugar sculptures, golden jelly,
pigs' bladders, and whale vomit (which was actually a great delicacy). The celebrations
lasted for nineteen days.

Make a Museum

You'll need

Pencil & paper

Art materials

Imagination

Have you visited any museums recently? In a museum, you'll find collections of objects that have been brought together for a reason. They might tell the story of someone's life, or the history of an invention.

GETTING STARTED

Decide what you'll put in your museum. You might choose to make a **set of tiny paintings or sculptures**. Or, you could look around and find **similar objects to group together** – like a collection of a particular kind of toy, or a group of rocks or shells.

HINTS AND TIPS

If you're making a set of pictures, remember to draw **frames**. You could invent **captions**, too – these are the labels beneath objects or artworks that contain all the information about what's on show.

Why not put on an **exhibition** for others to see? You could make a poster, tickets, and a visitor's guide so that your audience enjoy their museum experience!

You could copy work by famous artists or create your own original artwork to pin on the wall.

Or you might collect a set of everyday objects and display them in an interesting way.

DID YOU KNOW?

There are thousands of museums in the world. Some show exhibitions of paintings, sculpure, or other objects from history. Others present more unexpected collections – like the Museum of Instant Noodles in Osaka, Japan, or the Bread Museum in Ulm, Germany.

Stage a Sports Contest

You'll need

Friends

Outdoor space

Any sports equipment you can find!

Outdoor sports and games can be wild and wonderful. It's fun to compete with your friends! These games are best played in a park or garden where there's enough room to spread out.

GETTING STARTED

You'll need to ask some friends to join you! Together, make some notes on the sports you'd like to include in your contest. You might choose **traditional games** like running, jumping, skipping, or hopping. Or, you could dream up some more **unusual ideas** that combine several skills at once. Obstacle races are a good challenge for everyone!

HINTS AND TIPS

Draw up an **order of events**. Leave space to write down people's scores. Everyone could compete at once, or they could race one by one. You can use a **clock or stopwatch** to record people's times. Award points for style, too!

You could even invent more tricky events, like hula hooping while doing a crazy dance.

A long cane or stick can be used for high jump - or for limbo, where you pass under without your hands touching the floor!

DID YOU KNOW?

The first **Olympic Games** were held in Olympia, Greece in *776 BCE*. Athletes from different city-states challenged each other in competitions that included running, wrestling, discus, and chariot racing – and the winners were presented with crowns made of olive leaves. The games were held in honour of the Greek God, Zeus.

DRAW A NARWHAL

You'll need

Pencil & paper

The narwhal is a sea creature with a long horn like a unicorn. Follow these instructions to learn to draw it step-by-step!

GETTING STARTED

Take a **good look** at this picture of a narwhal. You're going to learn to draw it in three simple stages, following the pictures opposite. You'll discover that narwhals have:

- A rounded **body**
- A long **horn**, with a spiral pattern
- Some **tiny fins**, to help them swim around

HINTS AND TIPS

Narwhals live in the **cold waters** of the Arctic and **dive deep** to hunt for fish to eat. They love cod and halibut. You could draw your narwhal in action, searching for food!

1. Start with a simple shape. This looks like a smile, with some tiny leaves on the end.

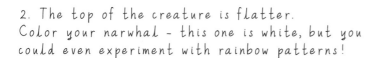

2. The top of the creature is flatter. Color your narwhal - this one is white, but you could even experiment with rainbow patterns!

3. Add the creature's long horn. It has a spiral pattern. You can add an eye, a mouth, and one fin toward the front of its body.

4. Make more step-by-step drawings! Everything is easier to draw when it's broken down into simple shapes.

DID YOU KNOW?

The **narwhal's horn** is actually a long tooth, and can grow up to three meters long. Narwhals were once hunted for their horns, which were believed to have magical powers. People thought narwhals were related to unicorns! In the 18th century, their horns were given pride of place in fashionable collections called 'Curiosity Cabinets', which were filled with rare shells, stuffed animals, and birds.

INVENT A YOGA POSE

You'll need

A yoga mat
or rug

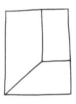

Space to move
around

A glass of
water

Yoga is a set of exercises, or poses, that help focus your mind and body. It encourages good posture, balance, and breathing.

GETTING STARTED

Sit down on your mat or rug, cross legged. You can **cross your legs** in a position called the **lotus**. A lotus is an Asian flower that grows on the surface of ponds and lakes. Take some deep breaths and relax! It's time to think about creating some different poses. Here are some ideas to get you started.

HINTS AND TIPS

The poses you invent don't have to be too complicated. Holding one arm up or one leg in the air is a great way of learning to balance. Once you've invented a pose, see if a friend can guess what it is.

Different yoga poses get all your muscles working, and move the blood around your body.

Dog

Snake

Star

Yoga poses are often named after animals, birds, or other things from the natural world. You might already know the dog, the snake, or the star pose.

DID YOU KNOW?

Yoga has been practised in Northern India for **thousands of years**. It's even mentioned in an ancient sacred text called the Rig Veda. The word 'yoga' means 'union' in the Sanskrit language. Many people recite **mantras** while doing yoga. This means they produce a sound like 'Om' or 'Um' as they concentrate on breathing.

make a story book quiz

You'll need

Pencil & paper

Your favorite books

A friend or two (or three!)

Do you have a book that you love more than any other? And a friend who feels the same? It's time to put your knowledge to the test!

GETTING STARTED

Choose a book you and a friend are confident that you know well. It's time to invent some questions for each other.

- Turn to a **random page**. Invent a question based on what you find there.
- Pick a **line** from the book. Who said it?
- Choose **a character** from the book (it could be someone who isn't in the story for long). Think of a question that involves them.

HINTS AND TIPS

Start with some **easy questions**, so your quiz gets off to a good start! After that, make your questions harder. If you want to make your quiz really tricky, set a **time limit**. After you've both quizzed each other, choose the best questions, and then find another friend to challenge.

You'll have more ideas about the questions you're going to invent as you search through the book. They could involve:

Your favorite characters.

The story or plot: What happened when?

You might invent a question about a location in the story - where the action takes place.

DID YOU KNOW?

The word '**quiz**' with the meaning that we understand today (a test of someone's knowledge) didn't appear in the dictionary until 1867. The invention of the radio in the 1920s and the introduction of television in people's homes in the 1950s made quizzes very popular. In the 1980s boardgames like Trivial Pursuit made quizzing even more of a craze.

CREATE A NEWSPAPER

You'll need

Pencil & paper

Newspapers – to inspire you

If you like investigating, recording, and writing, creating a newspaper could be the thing for you!

GETTING STARTED

Take a look at some newspapers. You may have some at home or at school. For your first creation, keep it simple! Start by **folding your piece of paper in half**. You'll have a front and back cover, and two pages inside to work with. You'll want to make your paper look like a real newspaper, so look at the examples opposite and notice:

– What a **front page** looks like.
– How the **text** is set out, and how **pictures** are included.

HINTS AND TIPS

– You could **interview** people and take **reporter's notes**.
– Your paper could be **handwritten**, or you could **type** articles and stick them in.
– You could produce your paper **monthly** or even **weekly**. Why not **make copies** for your friends at school?

You might want to follow this rough template.

You could give your paper a theme, like music or sport.

YOUR NEWSPAPER'S TITLE

price

HEADLINE IN BOLD TYPE!

By _____ (reporter's name)

Picture here - either a drawing or a photo!

With a caption underneath

You can set out your newspaper story in three columns, starting on the left-hand side.

Your article will continue in the middle column of the page.

And – finally – it will finish on the right-hand side!

You could write about what's been happening at home, but make it sound dramatic: KIDS HORRIFIED AT LACK OF BREAKFAST CEREAL FOR THIRD DAY IN ROW. Or, you could focus on events that have taken place at school or in your local area.

DID YOU KNOW?

The **first newspapers** were made of silk! They were made in **China** in the 8th century CE. News was collected every day, handwritten by scribes in the Imperial court, and copies were delivered to different parts of the country.

draw a self portrait

You'll need

Pencil & paper

A mirror

If you're not sure what to draw, you can always draw yourself! You'll learn to look closely - and you don't have to ask anyone to sit still and pose.

GETTING STARTED

How well do you know your face? Find a **mirror**, and look at your **features** carefully. Notice the shape of your eyes and brows, and their distance from the top of your head. Look at the position of your ears and the shape of your mouth.

HINTS AND TIPS

Start by sketching a **rough outline**. As a rule, faces are shaped like an oval, and divided so that the eyes, nose and mouth fall along the lines shown here. If you don't want to draw your whole face straight away you could practise **drawing separate parts** – just an eye, or just a nose!

Once you've mastered your face, try drawing your whole body. You could even include your pets or favorite books or your art materials in the picture.

Remember to sign and date the portrait! You could draw a new portrait every month - to chart how your looks change, and how different you feel.

DID YOU KNOW?

Mexican artist **Frida Kahlo** (1907–1954) began painting self-portraits at the age of 18 while she was in bed at home, recovering from an accident. She had a **mirror** fixed above her, and a family friend made her a **special easel** that she could rest on the bed. Frida often painted herself wearing traditional Mexican costumes, with flowers and ribbons in her hair.

KEEP A JOURNAL

You'll need

A notebook

Pens

Keeping a journal is great for making sense of the world! Writing things down helps you to focus, to think clearly, and to understand the way you feel.

GETTING STARTED

Keep a log of what you do at different times. Make notes on **where you've been** and **what you've spotted**. You don't have to write in your journal every day! Some weeks you'll feel like writing a lot, and other times you won't have much to record.

HINTS AND TIPS

Don't just write down the **exceptional things** – remember to include **everyday things** too. Note down what you do each day as if you were a **detective** watching someone else. What do you eat for breakfast? What do you do to relax? Keeping notes will help you remember what you were doing at this point in time far into the future. Years later, you'll look back at your notes and **remember your experiences** clearly.

Draw pictures and make lists in your journal. They'll help you describe what you've done each day in even more detail.

Use your journal for making plans and recording your favorite things. You can jot down the songs, books or games you love or write about what you'd like to be in the future.

DID YOU KNOW?

Journals are a great way of finding out how great thinkers of the past developed their ideas. **Charles Darwin** (1809–1882) worked out his theories of evolution in his many notebooks while traveling on his ship, the HMS Beagle; **Albert Einstein** (1879–1955) kept travel journals as well as filling books with his scientific ideas; while the notebooks belonging to scientist **Marie Curie** (1867–1934) are so radioactive they have to be kept in boxes lined with lead and viewed wearing protective clothing.

PUT ON A SHOW

You'll need

Friends

Some props

An audience

Create a show with your friends! You can mix music, magic, jokes, dance, and more. . .

GETTING STARTED

Gather your friends together, and **make a list** of what everyone can do. Does anyone have any **special skills** – like hula hooping or magic tricks? Can they sing or rap?

- Find a place to put on your show. It could be indoors or outdoors.
- Decide who is going to be your MC (or presenter). They will have to welcome everyone to the show, and announce the acts.

HINTS AND TIPS

- Keep it **varied**! Put different activities next to each other if you can.
- You **don't need special equipment**! Pots and pans can work for drums, cardboard boxes for props, a spoon for a microphone.

Encourage friends to share their talents - like playing an instrument or telling jokes.

Design a program for your show! You could also make tickets and a sign welcoming everyone.

DID YOU KNOW?

We know that our ancient ancestors entertained each other by performing **juggling tricks** as well as other **acrobatic feats**. Female jugglers are recorded on wall paintings in the 4,000-year-old tomb of Governor Baqet III (Egypt) while Chinese books tell of legendary sword juggler Lanzi, who performed 2,500 years ago while wearing long stilts. Don't try that at home!

MAKE A TIME CAPSULE

You'll need

Paper

Shoebox

Pencils

Fill a box with notes, pictures, and objects to record a particular moment in time.

GETTING STARTED

Choose a **small cardboard box** (a shoe box is perfect), and decorate it. You can paint it or cover it with pictures. Label the box with today's date. You could spend a few days **filling the box** with things that describe your life at this time.

HINTS AND TIPS

After you've filled your box (for some ideas, see opposite), **seal it with tape**, and **store it in a safe place**. If you like, you can label it with the date when you would like the box to be opened up again – it could be 20, 30, or 40 years in the future!

You might want to fill the box with your answers to the following questions:

How do you feel?

What have you done this week?

What's in the news?
(You could print or cut out articles from a newspaper, or ask an adult to help you write a summary of what's happening!)

You might want to draw yourself or include a photo.

You could write a story!

Add any objects you feel you can spare – like a small toy.

You could include notes on who you live with, and the names and personalities of your pets, if you have any.

DID YOU KNOW?

A time capsule is a group of **objects, recordings, or writings** that are stored safely to be opened at a later date. In 1939, two metal containers (guaranteed not to rust or decay for 5,000 years) were buried 50 feet below Flushing Meadows in New York. They held a selection of items chosen to describe American life in the 20th century, along with a collection of important texts, pictures, and news stories.

INVENT A typeface

You'll need

Pencil & paper
with lines or
a grid

A ruler

Some books

The design of a complete set of letters (their style, shape and thickness) is known as a TYPEFACE. Families of typefaces are called FONTS.

GETTING STARTED

Gather some books, and look at different styles of lettering. Notice how letters are formed! Most sit along a **baseline**. **Capital letters** and letters with **ascenders** (like f) are tall. Letters like p or y have **descenders**, which sit below the baseline.

Typeface

HINTS AND TIPS

When typeface designers **test out their creations**, they often write the sentence 'the quick brown fox jumps over the lazy dog' – because it contains **all 26 letters** of the alphabet!

SERIF typefaces look as if they have little tails at the end of each stroke.

Serif

SANS SERIF letters are made of simple lines that end without decoration.

Sans Serif

You could experiment with making your letters 3D, by adding shadows and edges.

DID YOU KNOW?

The 15th century saw the beginning of **book printing** on a huge scale. Workers called **typesetters** had the job of finding the individual metal letters and 'setting' them in the printing trays, to be covered with ink and printed onto paper. Capital letters were stored in one tray (**the upper case**), and small letters in another (**the lower case**). We still use those words to describe these different letter styles today!

Write a Song

Pencil & paper

A musical instrument, if you have one

Something to record on

Listening to songs makes us feel good - and writing them can feel great, too!

GETTING STARTED

Think about your favorite songs. What do you like about them? Think about the **lyrics** – what is the song about. Do the words **rhyme**? Next, there's the **melody** – is it catchy? Did you like it straight away, or did your love of the song creep up on you? Finally, there's the **beat** or **groove**. Does it make you want to dance? Or is it a slow song, that you like to relax and unwind to?

HINTS AND TIPS

There are many ways you could start – perhaps with the **words**, a **tune**, or just a **beat**. You don't have to compose everything at once. Keep a notebook handy at all times to record your thoughts. You could team up with friends, share ideas, and create your song together!

Pick a subject for your song!
A song can tell a whole story
or focus on something particular.
You might want to write a song
that describes the way you are
feeling today.

You could start by humming a
tune and finding words to fit.
Or by writing some lyrics and
working out a tune.

DID YOU KNOW?

The oldest written melody is over 3,400 years old! It was discovered carved into a piece of clay in the ancient city of Ugarit (modern-day Syria). The piece included instructions for playing the tune on the lyre (a stringed instrument rather like a harp).

IMPRESS YOUR FRIENDS

You'll need

Paper

Scissors

Hold up a piece of paper. Tell your friends that you are going to cut a hole in the middle and climb right through! Do they believe you?

GETTING STARTED

First, **fold your paper in half**. You're going to **take your scissors** and make cuts **along the red lines** shown in this diagram. You'll find step-by-step instructions on the opposite page.

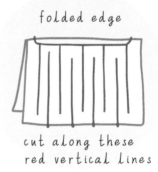

folded edge

cut along these red vertical lines

HINTS AND TIPS

Make sure you make the **first cut** and **vertical lines** in the right places. Don't snip too far, as it's easy to cut the paper in half. **Practise the steps** a few times before showing anyone – you'll want to be able to do them without thinking too hard! Once you've perfected this trick, try doing it with **smaller and smaller pieces of paper**. It's even more impressive!

Make the first cut
along the folded edge.

Cut zig-zags along the paper.

Start unfolding. . .

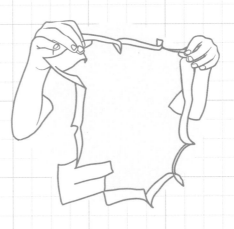

. . . and step through!

DID YOU KNOW?

You can't usually fold a regular piece of paper in half more than **seven times**. While you're playing with paper for this trick, give it a try! By the seventh fold, it will get too thick and be impossible to flatten. Challenge your friends to have a go!

create a cartoon

You'll need

Pencil & paper

Objects to
inspire you

To invent a cartoon character, start with
an animal, an object, and a few locations!

GETTING STARTED

Brainstorm your character! **Make a list** in three
columns, like the one opposite. You'll need
to decide **who** your character is, **what** their
personality is like and **where** they live. Write
down as many ideas as you can, so you have
plenty to choose from.

HINTS AND TIPS

Once you've chosen your cartoon character, sketch out your first thoughts.
- **Eyes** are important! You can express different emotions with eye and brow shapes.
- Give your characters a **catchphrase**! You'll want to decide if they're a hero, a villain, or something in between.
- Why not create a **comic strip** where they can get into all kinds of adventures!

CHARACTER BRAINSTORM

PERSONALITY	ANIMAL/OBJECT	LIVES
Bossy	Cereal packet	London
Very shy	Hamster	Underground
Crazy	Milkshake	On the street

A crazy milkshake

A very shy hamster

A bossy cereal packet

Develop your own style! You could make the outer lines very thick, or color everything bright blue.

DID YOU KNOW?

Comic strips (short picture stories, with text in speech bubbles or boxes) started appearing in American **newspapers** in the 19th century. Readers followed the adventures of characters like The Katzenjammer Kids (1897), or Little Nemo in Slumberland (1905). Superman started out as a daily newspaper comic strip in 1939.

INVENT A SECRET CODE

You'll need

Pencil & paper

A book you
and a friend
both own

Writing secret messages can be great fun! It's exciting to develop a code that only you and a friend can understand.

GETTING STARTED

Decide on a **short message** you'd like to send. The simplest kind of code is one where you **substitute** one set of letters for another, or **swap** letters for numbers.
– If A=1, B=2, C=3, D=4, E=5 (and so on), then the message 'PLEASE HELP ME' would read:

16-12-5-1-19-5 / 8-5-12-16 / 13-5

HINTS AND TIPS

Make sure your friends have instructions to decipher your codes. You can make codes that are even **trickier to crack**. If A=C, B=D, C=E, D=F, E=G, F=H, G=I, H=J, I=K, and so on, then the sentence 'INVENTING CODES IS FUN' would be:

KPXGPVKPI EQFGU KU HWP

Why not try a BOOK CODE! Find a book that you and a friend both own. It should be a chapter book, with lots of text on every page. The two books must be exactly the same – otherwise your code won't work.

First, write down your message on a piece of paper. To write it again using the secret code, search for the words you'd like to use among the pages of the book.

For each word, note down the page number followed by the paragraph number, the line number and finally the word number.

The word 'message' would be page 30, paragraph 1, line 1, word 5, and written 30-1-1-5.

The word 'codes' is page 31, paragraph 1, line 2, word 5, and written 31-1-2-5.

30

Once you get the hang of it, you can quickly create codes that can't be broken unless your friends know about the code book.

There are not many options for writing secret codes on these two short pages, but if you have a whole book to choose from, you'll find there are enough words to write very detailed messages to your friends!

31

Read the text on these two 'pages'. Can you decipher the hidden message?

The code is:

31-1-2-1
31-1-2-2
30-1-4-6
30-1-1-4
30-1-5-5
31-2-7-2
31-1-2-4
30-1-3-3
31-2-7-1

The answer is on page 71!

DID YOU KNOW?

Lemon juice is good for writing secret messages! It is invisible at room temperature, but the **carbon compounds** in the juice **oxidize** (and turn brown) on contact with **heat**. If you **shine a warm light bulb** on your lemon juice message, it will be revealed!

plan Your signature

You'll need

Pencil & paper

A good signature (the way you always sign your name) will last you a lifetime, and you'll enjoy signing your letters, papers, and artwork.

GETTING STARTED

Work out **what you like** in a signature! Do you want to write your full name, just part of it, or only your initials? Some signatures are **easy to read**, but you might prefer to **disguise your name** by using loops and squiggles.

HINTS AND TIPS

You could experiment with capital letters, underlining or even drawing a picture next to your name. Practise makes perfect – make sure you can write signature **the same way** every time!

You might choose flowing, looping lines, especially if you have double letters or Ts to cross.

lll eee tttttt

Some letters connect really easily. . .

Others are much trickier to make flow. . .

You can experiment with spiky, angular lines, or different spacing between your letters.

DID YOU KNOW?

The earliest form of the signature was the **seal**, invented 5,000 years ago by the Sumerian people. This official stamp, pressed into wet clay, showed who had written or agreed to a document.

sharpen your memory

You'll need

Pencil & paper

Some objects to remember

A stopwatch or timer

With a little practise (and some easy-to-learn methods) you can dramatically improve your power to remember things.

GETTING STARTED

Ask a friend to find **10–15 small objects** from around your home and set them up on a tray. They could be as small as a marble or as large as a book. Take a good look at the objects for around **3 minutes**. Then, take the tray away and see how many of them you can remember.

HINTS AND TIPS

A good way of remembering a group of objects or a set of facts is creating **pictures in your mind** that you can recall really easily. The **stranger or funnier** the pictures the better. If you want to remember a **large number** of objects, you'll have to find ways of grouping them together in an interesting way. By combining (or 'chunking') objects, you'll be able to remember more.

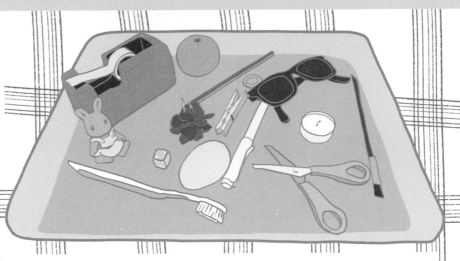

Let's imagine the following objects are set up on the tray. It's time to start creating some mind pictures!

You could begin by imagining a RABBIT wearing SUNGLASSES, cutting FLOWERS in a garden with SCISSORS. Next, you could picture an ORANGE and an EGG writing stories with a PEN and PENCIL by the light of a CANDLE. If you can recall just those two pictures, you'll already have remembered over half the objects on the tray.

Another trick is to remember just the first letter of each object. If you can spell out words with the letters, they will also trigger your memory. For instance, P-E-T: PEN, EGG, TOOTHBRUSH.

DID YOU KNOW?

Retrieving memories involves many **different parts of the brain**, but most new memories are made in a small area called the **hippocampus**. You're more likely to remember things if you **involve your senses** – particularly sight (by making pictures in your mind) and sound (by setting facts and lists to rhyme or music). To remember better, make notes! When you're writing, you're engaging your brain.

DESIGN A BUILDING

You'll need

Pencil & paper

Colored pens

Cardboard boxes (for a 3D model)

Architects design buildings. Why not invent one of your own! It could be floating in space or tunneling deep underwater.

GETTING STARTED

Think about:
- **What is your building for?** Is it a home, an office, a school – or something else?
- What are its **special features**?
- **Where in the world** is it?

HINTS AND TIPS

Your building doesn't have to be realistic!
Label the different parts of your building.
You could give it a name!

Your building might have a swimming pool on the roof.

It could feature a slide that connects one floor or one block with another.

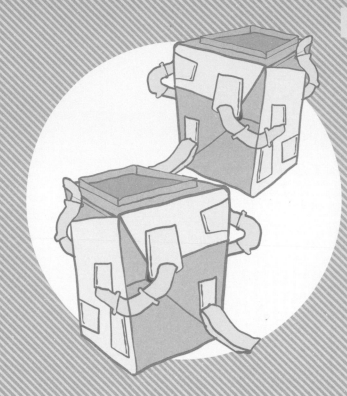

You could make your building from cardboard boxes or draw a floorplan showing how all the rooms connect.

DID YOU KNOW?

The tallest building in the world is the **Burj Khalifa** in Dubai, in the United Arab Emirates. It's made of steel and glass – so much that a team of window cleaners is constantly working. Once they've finished, they have to start all over again.

MAKE A LIST

You'll need

Pencil & paper

Colored pens

When you're trying to work something out, it's a good idea to make a list of all your plans.

GETTING STARTED

It's fun to make lists at **any time of the year**! You could make lists of:
- Tasks that need doing immediately.
- Things you'd like to do in the future.
- Books, songs, or films you enjoy.

HINTS AND TIPS

Make your list **look good**! Take time to draw grids, boxes, and other shapes. You can use colored pens and pencils too!

First, make your list look good!

Write each task in a circle.

You can use colors to code your list, and lines to connect one task with another.

And cross tasks off as you complete them.

Write thank-yous

Homework (write story)

Feed cat

Clean out hamster

Tidy bedroom

Organize books

Fold clothes

A larger circle around a group of items means they are all connected.

DID YOU KNOW?

Our brains love lists! Lists help us to **organize information** and **remember things** we might otherwise forget. The act of creating a list – or completing tasks on a list – makes us feel happy. It's good to make your tasks short and achievable – breaking larger ones down into smaller actions.

create a book cover

You'll need

Pencil & paper

Some books, for inspiration

Book covers are bold, exciting - and fun to design!

GETTING STARTED

You could **design a cover** for an **imaginary book of your own** or create a new cover for a **book that you already own**.

- Make a list of all the things you want to get across on the cover.
- What's exciting about it?
- If it's a story, who are the main characters?
- What pictures can you use to sum up the book?

HINTS AND TIPS

Following the plan opposite, sketch out your cover. It's good to use **large type** for the title – so it can be spotted from a distance. You'll need to write a **blurb** for the back cover, summing up the book in an exciting way (without giving away the ending)!

Back cover

Front cover

Title

Blurb

The blurb tells you what you're going to find in the book!

WHAT CAN I DO?

Illustration

Mary Richards

Publisher's logo

Barcode

Spine

Author's name

Your cover should be bold and eye-catching. It's good to give the reader a sense of the exciting world they are about to enter!

DID YOU KNOW?

Early **books** didn't have covers at all. They were written on **papyrus** (made from reeds), **parchment** (made from animal skin) or **silk** – and rolled into **scrolls**. The first bound books were covered with wood or leather. The most precious versions were even stamped with gold and jewels.

PLAY TOWN AND COUNTRY

You'll need

Pencil & paper

Friends to
play with

In this simple game, players try to outwit each othe
by thinking of unique people, places, and things.

GETTING STARTED

Give everyone a piece of paper. Together, **choose the categories**
you're going to play the game with. Here are some ideas – and you
could add more to the list, too!

– Town or city   – Vegetable
– Country   – Book
– Animal   – Film

Next, **choose a letter of the alphabet**. The game begins! Everyone
writes down something in each category beginning with that letter.
Set a time limit, then share your answers. Score a point for
each original answer – but no points if two people have the same word!

HINTS AND TIPS

Some letters are easier than others. Don't pick **X, Y, or Z** – you won't think be able to think of
many examples! When you're playing, try to guess what your friends are going to write and pick
something different.

There are thousands of cities and towns in the world! Start by thinking of places you've visited.

Impress your friends by picking an unusual animal, like a Capybara or an Aardvark.

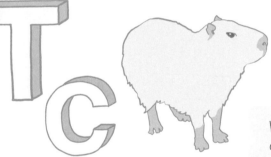

When thinking of a book, don't count THE for T or A for A.

Look around the room you're in. There might be books on the shelves or objects that give you ideas!

DID YOU KNOW?

The only **country** that begins with the letter O is Oman, and Qatar is the only Q. However, there are eighteen countries beginning with the letter C and twenty-five that start with the letter S. See how many you can name!

relax and daydream

You'll need

Imagination

A quiet space

It can be relaxing to empty your mind of all the things you usually spend time thinking about.

GETTING STARTED

Find a **quiet, calm space**. You might want to sit back in a chair or lie down on the floor. Close your eyes. Take some deep breaths, concentrating on the movement of your ribs as they rise and fall.

Next, imagine a place where **good things** are happening. You could put yourself in that place, or invent new characters and decide what they would do there.

HINTS AND TIPS

You don't have to spend a long time on this activity. Even **five minutes** can be relaxing! When you next have time, return to the same scene, and carry on with your daydream.

Your daydream might take place in a home very different to yours.

You might like to imagine a scene at a school just like yours.

You could imagine yourself in the future.

It could be fun to set your daydream in a place you've been on vacation, or somewhere you've always wanted to travel.

DID YOU KNOW?

When you **breathe in**, your lungs fill with air. They help you absorb the oxygen you need to keep your body working. You **breathe out** carbon dioxide. Breathing deeply allows your body to take in more oxygen.

SOME MORE IDEAS

You've created, planned, made, drawn, and invented - congratulations! We hope you've enjoyed all the suggestions in this book and that you'll be keen to make up your own activities based on the things inside it.

What will you do next?

If you've enjoyed a particular game or activity, can you think of a **variation**? For instance, if you completed **Invent a Typeface** (page 47) you could try spelling out a word using objects. See how many examples you can find – an orange could be an O, a pencil could be an I, a piece of string could loop into an S, and so on.

If you had fun with **Make a Den** (page 21), you could try creating a den outdoors. For your outdoor den, you could make a frame with long branches, and make the walls from leaves and twigs. You might need string to tie them together. If it's dry, you can bring out some of the cushions, pillows, or blankets from your indoor den.

If **Create a Secret Code** (page 55) was your favorite activity, you might want to make further codes by inventing your own symbols for letters. With a friend, you could create a new alphabet of signs that no-one else can decipher. It might help to work out a way of remembering your symbols. Your letter B could be shaped a little like a banana, or P a pen. Did you crack the code on page 55? The answer is 'you can use your book to create secret messages'.

Fill a notebook with all your plans and ideas – it will come in handy next time you ask the question 'What Can I Do?'

Finally, we'd love to see your notes, your pictures and your inventions – do send them to us! You can tag us on Instagram @agnesandaubrey or write to us via our website at www.agnesandaubrey.com, where we'd love to feature your thoughts and plans.

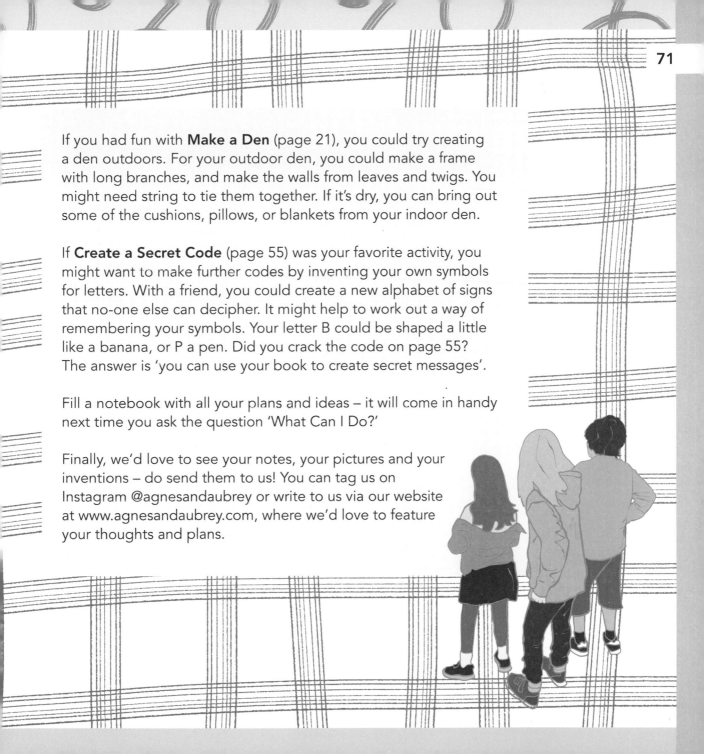

Published in 2022 by
Agnes & Aubrey
1st Floor, Unit D,
Emperor House, Dragonfly Place
London SE4 2FL

agnesandaubrey.com
hello@agnesandaubrey.com

Design by Agnes & Aubrey, and Emily Sear
hiyamate.com

A catalogue record of this book is available from the British Library.

ISBN 978-1-9168816-0-0 (North American edition)
ISBN 978-1-9168816-1-7 (UK edition)

Printed in China on paper from responsible sources.

This edition distributed in North America by
Consortium Book Sales & Distribution, Inc.,
part of the Ingram Content Group

Agnes & Aubrey would like to thank:
David, Arlo, Zubin, Quincy, and Viola Schweitzer
Becky Overton, Oscar, and Freddie Burgess
Poppy Andrews and Dave Walsh
Katherine Bright-Holmes, Ellen Myrick, Elizabeth Sadzik, and Emily Sear